# 300 ARGUMENTS

Also by Sarah Manguso

*Ongoingness*
*The Guardians*
*The Two Kinds of Decay*
*Hard to Admit and Harder to Escape*
*Siste Viator*
*The Captain Lands in Paradise*

# 300 ARGUMENTS

SARAH MANGUSO

Graywolf Press

Parts of this book were previously published in slightly different forms in the *Believer,* the *New York Ghost,* the *New York Times Book Review,* the *Paris Review,* and *Unsaid.*

This publication is made possible, in part, by the voters of Minnesota through a Minnesota State Arts Board Operating Support grant, thanks to a legislative appropriation from the arts and cultural heritage fund, and through a grant from the Wells Fargo Foundation. Significant support has also been provided by Target, the McKnight Foundation, the Amazon Literary Partnership, and other generous contributions from foundations, corporations, and individuals. To these organizations and individuals we offer our heartfelt thanks.

Published by Graywolf Press
250 Third Avenue North, Suite 600
Minneapolis, Minnesota 55401

www.graywolfpress.org

Published in the United States of America
Printed in Canada

ISBN 978-1-55597-764-1

2  4  6  8  9  7  5  3  1
First Graywolf Printing, 2017

Library of Congress Control Number: 2016937638

Cover design: Kyle G. Hunter

# 300 ARGUMENTS

A great photographer insists on writing poems. A brilliant essayist insists on writing novels. A singer with a voice like an angel insists on singing only her own, terrible songs. So when people tell me I should try to write this or that thing I don't want to write, I know what they mean.

———

You might as well start by confessing your greatest shame. Anything else would just be exposition.

———

It can be worth forgoing marriage for sex, and it can be worth forgoing sex for marriage. It can be worth forgoing parenthood for work, and it can be worth forgoing work for parenthood. Every case is orthogonal to all the others. That's the entire problem.

———

I wrote my college application essay about playing in a piano competition, knowing I would lose to the kid who had played just before me. *Even while I played knowing I would lose,* I wrote, *still I played to give the judges something to remember.* I pretended my spasms of self-regard transcended the judges' informed decisions about the pianists who were merely the best. I got into college.

———

I assume the cadets are gay, but then I see they are merely unafraid of love. They are preparing to go to war, and with so little time to waste, they say what they mean.

———

At faculty meetings I sat next to people whose books had sold two million copies. Success seemed so close, just within reach. On subway benches I sat next to people who were gangrenous, dying, but I never thought I'd catch what they had.

———

What's worse: Offending someone or lying to someone? Saying something stupid when it's your turn, or not saying anything? Tell me which, and I'll tell you your problem.

———

The trouble with comparing yourself to others is that there are too many others. Using all others as your control group, all your worst fears and all your fondest hopes are at once true. You are good; you are bad; you are abnormal; you are just like everyone else.

———

Some people ditch friends and lovers because it's easier to get new ones than to resolve conflicts with the old ones, particularly if resolving a conflict requires one to admit error or practice mercy. I'm describing an asshole. But what if the asshole thinks he's ditching an asshole?

———

Inner beauty can fade, too.

———

The waterbirds near my house are in middle school. The coots' voices crack; the seagulls bully the ducks; the egret just got braces and stands, humiliated, by himself.

———

Many bird names are onomatopoetic—they name themselves. Fish, on the other hand, have to float there and take what they get.

———

I used to avoid people when I was afraid I loved them too much. Ten years, in one case. Then, after I had been married long enough that I was married even in my dreams, I became able to go to those people, to feel that desire, and to know that it would stay a feeling.

———

In a dream my friend and I begin the act and both immediately want it to be over, but we have to continue, impelled by some obscure reason. I wake wondering whether we could ever enjoy it. I think about it all day, really dedicate myself to it. I think about it for two more days, and that's how I fall in love with my friend.

———

Like a vase, a heart breaks once. After that, it just yields to its flaws.

———

In the morning I wake amid fading scenes of different characters, different settings, all restatements of that first desire, a ghost who haunts me as the beauty he was at sixteen.

———

My friend learns Chinese and moves to China, but her limited vocabulary is good for grocery shopping, not for falling in love. When her heart breaks she is obliged to ask, *Why won't you fuck me?*

———

I've put horses in poems, but I've never ridden one. They just seem like such a good thing to put into literature.

———

Biographies should also contain the events that failed to foreshadow.

———

*Facility* means *prison* (building), *lifelessness* (art), or *grace* (athletes). Within a gesture of apparent perfection, a mortal heart must beat.

———

I remember a girl who was famous in school for having woken from a drunken blackout and said to whoever was there, *Are you my judges?*

———

In real life, my healthy boyfriend said that he envied my paralytic disease—that I'd earned the right to a legitimate nervous breakdown. A few years later he was in an accident and became paralyzed from the neck down. That's just bad writing.

———

It isn't so much that geniuses make it look easy; it's that they make it look fast.

———

Of a page of perfect prose I read in a dream, I remember only this: *"Thank you," she said. Her simple answer concealed the truth.*

———

The man who had me in a phone booth married quickly after the affair ended. His novel had everything in it—the phone booth, the shame, the sash he sewed to wear over the surgical appliance in his belly. In the novel it covers a plaster leg cast. The front page of his website is a glowing glass phone booth standing alone in snow. The book got bad reviews. He has two children.

———

I never joined Facebook because I want to preserve my old longings. And also yours.

———

We like stories that are false and seem true (realist novels), that are true and seem false (true crime), that are false and seem false (dragons and superheroes), or that are true and seem true, but it's harder to agree on what that is.

———

The fastest way to revise a piece of work is to send it, late at night, to someone whose opinion you fear. Then rewrite it, praying you'll finish in time to send a new version by morning.

———

Having a worst regret betrays your belief that one misstep caused all your undeserved misfortune.

————

I don't write long forms because I'm not interested in artificial deceleration. As soon as I see the glimmer of a consequence, I pull the trigger.

————

My teacher cried while I listened. None of his books had ever made money, not even the famous one, he said. He'd spent his life trying to write perfect books, and when he tried to make money, he couldn't. I didn't think I'd ever feel as old as he seemed at that moment, but here we are.

————

The difference between writers under thirty and writers over forty is that the former, like everyone their age, already know how to act like famous people: people whose job it is to be photographed.

———

I wish I could ask the future whether I should give up or keep trying. Then again, what if trying, even in the face of certain failure, feels as good as accomplishing? What if it's even better? And here we are again.

———

Horror is terror that stayed the night.

———

I can't bear to think of my dead friend, but I don't mind rereading a few things that have nothing to do with him and that always move me to tears. The grief reservoir empties to a manageable level. In this way I can mourn him without having to think about him.

————

There will come a time when people decide you've had enough of your grief, and they'll try to take it away from you.

————

You'll never know what your mother went through.

————

I've known a few people who approached the act as a perfectible art. I've known some great perverts, too. Others were in love. Desire abandoned them all. It's the ones I didn't fuck, or didn't fuck enough, or haven't fucked enough, that I still dream about.

————

In ninth grade I was too afraid to speak to the boy I loved, so I mailed him a black paper heart every week for a year. I wasn't afraid of him; I was afraid of my feeling. It was more powerful than God. If we'd ever spoken it might have burned the whole place down.

———

Shame needs an excuse to feel ashamed. It apologizes for everything, even itself.

———

I've never seen a ghost and I don't believe in them. I might see one tonight, but even then I wouldn't believe in ghosts. I'd believe in that ghost.

———

Just before the poetry reading starts, I ask the overgrown boy sitting next to me why he likes poetry, what happened to him, and he says, *I went to war.*

———

The affair is over, but at least things have gone somewhere, if only into oblivion. And maybe oblivion is what I wanted all along.

———

The dark owns everything, but our sun comes out often enough that we think the universe is half dark, half light.

———

When the worst comes to pass, the first feeling is relief.

———

Rock faces, bodies of water, the crotch of a tree. It's harder to personify the sky.

———

Bad art is from no one to no one.

———

Talking with someone who reveals nothing, I hear myself madly filling the emptiness with information about myself.

———

Your deathbed self floats out of the time machine to tell you that everything will be fine. Your kindergarten self floats out and asks you to tell her the same thing. Imagine them standing hand in hand, waiting for you to choose between them.

———

I write in defense of the beliefs I fear are least defensible. Everything else feels like homework.

———

Our fifth-grade class assembled cat skeletons from bags of bones and blocks of red-brown plasticine. One of my friends worked on the vertebrae, hastily sticking the clay between them. I worked on the jaw, just that one joint, trying to align the two bones perfectly. Even when I was ten I wanted to master one small thing. When I think I should change, I remember that I've never really changed, might never need to.

———

Finally, a form I'll always have time to write—but of course it demands more than time.

———

Perfection and beauty overlap, but incompletely.

———

While I lie on the table, studded with needles, the energy of my body swells beyond my body and into a halo, about four inches out into the room, just barely distinguishing me from the rest of the world.

———

With great and solemn portent, my teacher announced she would tell us something that her teacher had told her, and that her teacher's teacher had told him, and so on, back to Yeats: *The thing to remember is that no one ever finds out that you don't know what you're doing.* My other teacher, after I asked him a contrived question about nothing, paused and very kindly said, *The thing to remember is that I only have about thirty-five, forty years left to live.*

———

My least favorite received idea about writing is that one must find one's voice, as if it's there inside you, ready to be turned on like a player piano. Like character, its very existence depends on interaction with the world.

———

*But don't forget—they pay by the pound!* says my friend who is well compensated for writing long books and is teaching me how to get paid more for mine.

———

Faced with a camera lens, hideously overwitnessed, I immediately start trying to impersonate myself.

———

Picture a locked storeroom strewn with all the old sheet music I had to give back to music teachers and choral directors, paper lying unused for decades, fading yellow, annotated in sharp pencil, the pages containers of such joy that it sometimes choked me silent. No one who picks it up could know how it saved my life, over and over.

———

The trouble with letting people see you at your worst isn't that they'll remember; it's that you'll remember.

———

I knew I was getting somewhere when I finished writing a book and didn't think, *It isn't my fault that my ill health prevented me from perfecting this* but instead thought, *Well, this is the best I could do.*

After I stopped hoping to outgrow them, my fears were no longer a burden. Hope is what made them a burden.

———

When my husband does the dishes he always leaves some platter in the sink, some surface unwiped. I tried to correct the behavior until I remembered that if I finish everything in my *Work in Progress* folder I'm afraid I'll die.

———

My first dozen romances weren't interesting because I wasn't learning anything because I was trying so hard not to. I was trying to stop time.

———

After I publish an autobiographical essay, men accuse me of having tried and failed to present myself as likable, and women accuse me of having tried and failed to represent them.

———

*I can't believe this is happening,* I thought the first time we fucked, fourteen years ago, and keep thinking. We married other people, had children. I still can't believe it. I might never believe it.

———

I don't love writing; I love having a problem I believe I might someday write my way out of.

———

I read three-hundred-year-old graffiti at Eton and six-hundred-year-old graffiti at a castle in Urbino, but the carvings on my high school's walls were more exciting. The seventies! The sixties! I could just about see them out of the corner of my eye as they drifted offstage and into history.

———

The smallest and shortest pieces of art strive for perfection; the largest and longest strive for greatness.

———

I don't feel lonely as I work, but when I look out the window next to my desk, I frequently mistake strangers walking up or down the block for people I know.

———

Slowly, slowly, I accumulate sentences. I have no idea what I'm doing until suddenly it reveals itself, almost done.

———

I hate wasting time and I hate wasting space. I hate chatting and I hate clutter. In college I was once accused of owning only six objects. In my dating days, as soon as I anticipated going to bed with someone, it seemed absurd, irrational, to further resist the inevitable. If there's a good line in a book, I will copy out the line and sell the book.

———

Even if I'm writing for no audience, I'm appealing to the audience of all who ever agreed that *A* is *A*: all readers who have ever lived.

———

With ten minutes left in the exam period, I write my best sentence. Holding out for an even better one, I write nothing for the remaining nine.

———

When we agree that *A* sounds like *A*, we're not just acceding to an abstract system; we're agreeing with people who were like us, joking around, making stuff up. The jokes are lost, but their artifacts remain in the system.

———

It takes $x$ hours to write a book and some percentage of $x$ hours to wish I were a different writer, writing a different book.

———

To call a piece of writing a fragment, or to say it's composed of fragments, is to say that it or its components were once whole but are no longer.

———

A woman starts a rumor that I slept with a man in another woman's bed. Fifteen years later I look her up on the Internet and find three DUI mug shots. In the first she's the pretty redhead I remember from college, maybe a few cracks in the veneer, but in the last one she's obese, ruined. I still don't forgive her. I pity her, but I won't forgive her just for being pitiable. Hating her is an act of respect.

———

I sat at my college desk, looked out the window at the three church spires, pretended it was the nineteenth century, and felt privately embarrassed. I remember the embarrassment better than I remember the view.

———

The first beautiful songs you hear tend to stay beautiful because better than beauty, which is everywhere, is the memory of first discovering beauty.

———

The letter *Q* is rare in English, but in French, it's nothing special. Whenever I have to use another language, I realize I've characterized the letters of the alphabet by their frequency in English. These occult characterizations are part of the Englishness of my very thoughts.

———

Details aren't automatically interesting.

———

I'd like to meet someone whose passage through life has been continuous, whose life has happened to an essential self, and not been just a series of lives happening to a series of selves.

———

In a long relationship, you learn exactly what to do to get each other off. It becomes mechanical. But you also learn exactly what to do to enrage each other. It becomes mechanical. The pleasures of a long relationship are the things that you never quite learn about the other—the ways in which you remain strangers.

———

I feared he'd drag me across the country again, so I railed against California. He feared I'd never leave New York again, so he railed against New York. We each feared the other would refuse to negotiate, so in the face of imaginary approaching trains, we sent out opposing trains, meeting perceived unreasonableness with equal or greater unreasonableness.

———

The full moon is saying *O!* But the sun is silent.

———

Am I happy? Damned if I know, but give me a few minutes and I'll tell you whether you are.

———

Sometimes the bedroom light goes on and off three times fast. It turns on in the night. The fan starts and stops. I was angry at the ghost for months, would shout at it to stop trying to scare me. Now I understand it's just lonely.

———

It's easier to speak to a crowd, to stare into the spotlight, than it is to look into a human face.

———

Who seems a harmless fool to those above him is a malevolence to those beneath.

———

Everyone considers some part of his own life a universally applicable model, and I'm no exception.

———

When someone insults you, it will infuriate him if you pretend to misunderstand the insult as a compliment.

———

Interesting people aren't interested in appearing interesting.

———

A friend visits with a basket in each hand, her twin sons. She feeds them, changes them, carries them, and lays them down with perfunctory attention. She says, *Sometimes I think, "It's been seven months! Where in the world is their mother?"*

———

Some people love only those they can condescend to, those they can tenderly despise.

———

Assume that the most annoying person you know, the one who won't leave you alone, is in love with you.

———

I want to ask the happiest person in the world whether it was worth it, all the sacrifices he made in order to become so happy.

———

Your pet represents your human partner. It also represents you.

———

The true nobility put their inferiors at ease—by being kind to them? No, by dismantling the system for a moment.

———

When I confessed my age he asked, *Are you married?* When I kissed him goodnight he said, *Again!* and I kissed him again and he begged me to come out with him and his backwoods friends on the last night of their once-in-a-lifetime trip to the city. Sincerity that pure was impossible to include in my life then, and I had to turn away. It was like looking at the sun.

———

The first time you love someone who doesn't love you back it seems wrong, not morally but logically, a river flowing up a mountain. How can such a feeling be wrong? You'll return to that very river, as many times as it takes.

———

Outsiders pretend to be insiders, and it makes them unlikable. Insiders pretend to be outsiders, and we love to play along.

———

The most likable person you know just might be a sociopath.

———

Parental love is a one-way, all-consuming love, like a crush that asks nothing of its object. You can inhabit it totally, and no one will try to heal you of it.

———

My mind contains a deck of cards, one for each person I've ever desired, and for each dream it draws one at random. The trouble is that when I wake up, I take the dream literally.

———

A nonspecific wish to change the world isn't about the world. It's about you.

———

I've written whole books in order to avoid writing other books.

———

One must be able to empathize with a suicide yet not become one.

———

The well adjusted seem to distribute their fear across their lives, not just keep it in one area, so it seems to disappear.

———

My husband sees the apartment as a series of particulate spaces and moments, but I see it as one entity, so we disagree about its tidiness.

———

Whatever you're feeling, billions already have. Feel for them.

———

It's interesting to watch my friend speak carefully about what he thinks I'll find interesting.

———

Some people will punish you merely for witnessing their weakness. Even if they sought you out and asked for help. Even if you helped. Especially if you helped.

———

A woman I knew was so attached to the idea of having a terrible secret, she told me the same secret three times, each time as if for the first time.

———

Some people care most about exhibiting how much they care.

———

Preferable to accepting one's insignificance is imagining the others hate you.

———

My teacher told us about having to sort a box of objects in a psychiatric research experiment. An alarm rang; his time was up. The test was designed to measure how long it took for subjects to declare the objects unsortable. My teacher was so proud. He said it meant he had schizophrenic tendencies.

———

A false compliment can land if the recipient wishes it were true.

———

*I didn't do it for the money,* says my friend who appeared in a pornographic film. *I did it for the shame.*

———

You can choose your friends but not your friendships.

———

I kiss his hand. I say my name, and he kisses mine. A few minutes later we're next to each other in the smaller of two rooms, the smoke tracing rococo curls. I'm not talking about fucking; I'm talking about intimacy. One used to fade into the other, and sometimes I forget I've learned the difference.

———

Among those with less, I try to distract them from the imbalance. Doing so feels like theft. Among those with more, I try to distract them from the imbalance. Doing so feels like charity.

———

Thank heaven I don't have my friends' problems. But sometimes I notice an expression on one of their faces that I recognize as secret gratitude.

———

Today, for the first time, I sent a fan letter to someone younger than I am. It marks a change in my relationship to the world.

———

Keeping a debt is a gift to the giver: it renders him generous.

———

*Compare and despair,* intone the self-help bibles. But without anyone to compare myself to, how would I know what constitutes a human life?

———

In twenty years I have had four students who could listen with superhuman attention. All of them were dancers.

———

Is it a failure of my imagination that I've never been able to summon any genuine feeling about a sports team? I'm lying—the Red Sox, 2004, postseason. But that was the only time. And it was an affectation of someone else's enthusiasm.

———

There must be birds that sing or fly better or worse than other birds of their species; I've never noticed any. But the birds have.

———

People congregate according to their relative levels of luck.

———

When I meet the movie star we're both alone, eating rice balls at the bar. His beauty is outrageous. We walk out together into a blinding summer afternoon.

We keep talking as he drives. Maybe he tells me he likes my crooked teeth. We part and never meet again. My husband thinks these fantasies are absurd. *I just imagine fucking someone I meet somewhere.* But he doesn't understand. If I imagined fucking someone I met somewhere, before I knew it we might really be fucking.

———

Two men spend all their time together. One buys a trampoline for the children; the other arranges a cooking contest. Parlor games are played nightly with the wives. One night one man feels superior; the next night, the other. Everyone is unhappy. The men are the unhappiest of all, but if they avoided each other they would be even unhappier, never knowing where they stood.

———

The boy realizes that if he can feed a toy dog a cracker, he can just as easily feed a toy train a cracker. That if he can feed a toy dog from a bottle, he can just as easily feed a cracker from a bottle.

———

No point in trying to explain myself to those who refuse to understand. I've already lost that game.

———

I annotated my friend's book manuscript with scribbles on every page. She annotated mine with a single note: *This needs to be better.* She trusted that I would know what to do, and I did.

———

Fewer villains leave boot prints on their victims than simply deny their relative luck.

———

If you want to know someone's secret, don't ask a thing. Just listen.

———

The best gift is unexpected but not ostentatiously so, or it will seem as if the giver is soliciting praise. Some people always give excellent gifts. It is a talent. A gift. Unteachable.

———

Is it more satisfying when someone finally finds the itch in the middle of your back, or when you just reach up and scratch it yourself on the first try? It depends on your erotics of helplessness.

———

Vices have much in common with their corresponding virtues.

———

The most fervent kiss of my life was less than five seconds long more than ten years ago with someone else's husband. It still hasn't quite worn off.

———

When my husband travels I miss him terribly. On the first day I tidy his clutter, clean his whiskers from the sink, gather his papers into a pile. It's as if I'm trying to clean up a crime scene and leave nothing for the cops to find.

———

There are two kinds of people: those who can't perform the act when they're sad and those who perform it only to escape sadness. I have a theory that the second kind of person lives longer.

———

What's more exciting than an affair? Knowing the other's willingness to have an affair.

———

Sometimes a single sentence can be enough to fill the imagination completely. And sometimes a book's title is enough.

———

The aftershocks of the first time last forever. One might take this as permission not to finish anything.

———

There were people I wanted so much before I had them that the entire experience of having them was grief for my old hunger.

———

I've taken on bad habits in order to grow closer to certain others—watching an inane television show, playing a video game, drinking. The habits lasted, but I never minded because they weren't mine. They were just affectations of other people's.

———

Crying turns to laughing and laughing to crying—if the storm is intense enough, all the fuses in the house blow.

———

Before I'd ever had sex, I claimed that music was better than sex, and I knew I was right. It's a better accompaniment for longing.

———

Anger conceals pain. It also conceals love.

———

One chair upon another is pornographic. Ten in a stack is aspirational.

———

I made so many mistakes on purpose just to get them out of the way.

———

One cannot convince another to love anything or anyone. Better than arguing is just pointing and saying *Look at that*.

———

I've committed greater perversions with some of my exes than I have with my husband. They used to provide absolute proof of an extreme love, proof I no longer need.

———

Judgments and feelings are incompatible and inextricable.

———

When an ex writes from out of the blue and wants to have dinner while he's in town, it's because he got married. Years later, when he writes from out of the blue and wants to have dinner while he's in town, it's because he got divorced.

———

I don't think the lover ever forgets who started out as the beloved.

———

How to make sex irrelevant to the story: make the narrator frigid. But then it becomes the story.

———

I fell in love with someone who wanted to keep pining away in private, and he resented me for ruining that.

———

*If you can't be with the one you love,* my friend says, *love the one who looks like the one you love.* Other people call this having a type. It's an expression of grief for an original loss.

———

We hide in plain sight, in our bodies.

———

I keep some desires unfulfilled for fear of losing all desire, but sometimes I need a break from them anyway.

———

Nothing is more boring to me than the re-re-restatement that language isn't sufficiently nuanced to describe the world. Of course language isn't enough. Accepting that is the starting point of using it to capacity. Of increasing its capacity.

———

Dying young can really help an art career along. It's the careerist's ultimate paradox.

———

I read your work hoping to find flaws. I stop reading it, fearing its perfection.

———

My favorite jokes are either the simplified restatement of a received obfuscation or onstage glee followed by offstage disappointment. But knowing that doesn't make me able to write jokes any more than having an idea for a story makes me able to tell one.

———

I used to write these while playing hooky on what I hoped would be my magnum opus. Assigning myself to write three hundred of them was like forcing myself to chain-smoke until I puked, but it didn't work. I didn't puke.

———

For me the greatest thrill of Rome was walking into the Forum, picking up a piece of ancient stone where it lay, and dropping it somewhere else.

———

The phrase *great woman* sounds strange because it's seldom used outside the phrase *Behind every great man is a great woman.*

———

The title of a book seems so important before I commit to it, but my favorite titles don't belong to my favorite books, and my favorite books transcend their titles as movie stars transcend their human names.

———

Dutch dikes *(dijks)* are arranged in threes—*watchers, sleepers,* and *dreamers,* named thus by their proximity to the water.

———

The word *fragment* is often misused to describe anything smaller than a bread box, but an eight-hundred-page book is no more complete or unbroken than a ten-line poem. That's confusing size with integrity. An ant is not a fragment of an elephant except orthographically.

———

*Rest* is the term used to describe the mind's retreat to the background of consciousness. But one must control the attention exquisitely, without giving too much to the immediate surroundings or to things of the imagination, without overtraining the focus, without getting sleepy. It's hard work, learning how to rest like this.

———

Aspiring to fame is aspiring to a life of small talk.

———

People like to tell my very successful friend that they, too, intend to write some books. He always answers, with big eyes and a ghoulish smile, *How hard could it be?*

———

Envy is a narrative impulse: if I got what I wanted, what would happen then?

———

There are no memories, just artifacts. And they're all lying.

———

Certainty is the opposite of thinking; I'm certain of it.

———

Mothers must have sung to their babies before there was such a thing as music. I wonder what they thought of it, how they understood it, that singing.

———

Another friend always gives the same consolation to those afraid of publishing some potentially embarrassing passage. *Don't worry*, he whispers beatifically. *No one will read it.*

———

I like writing that is unsummarizable, a kernel that cannot be condensed, that must be uttered exactly as it is.

———

Nouns are exciting because of their variety and specificity, but consider the amazing capacity of the humble pronoun.

———

I keep three kinds of books: those I want to read, those I want to reread, and those I want to reopen just to confirm how bad they are.

———

An adjective is comparative, but so is a noun; an apple is something that isn't anything but an apple. It helps to remember this when tempted to use an adjective.

———

It's so boring to be a soprano, shackled to the melody, ineluctably noticed.

———

Great artists make work like the *os innominatum*, the unnamed bone, called thus in the first edition of *Gray's Anatomy*, for its resemblance to no known object, but they do it incidentally.

———

No one can steal something that's too small to see.

———

Death will reveal what you would otherwise have finished. Also what you never would have finished. I found the notes for a book a woman had been working on for thirty years: sixteen pages.

———

Every new routine begins in desperation. And ends in a different desperation.

———

Overheard in the café: *Get me one of those cheese sandwiches—Capri? You know, like the island where Tiberius died?*

———

Every few years I decide I'll write something purely for money, and I work on it for a long time. Then I wrap its carcass in plastic and seal it in a container and hide it under the house.

———

After a friend dies young, the story of her life becomes the exposition to a tragedy. This is the central problem of biography.

———

More bad writing from real life: I tried to run into someone every day for four months, then gave up. Four days later I ran into him without trying. Four hours later, I ran into him again and we went to a diner and shared a slice of pie.

———

In the long moment after I complete a project, adrift on a windless sea, I return to the idea of a certain imaginary book I'll never write, a goal I'll never reach. As soon as I think of a new project, I push the imaginary book far ahead of me, past the horizon, where it will wait for me until I need it again.

———

A famous writer publishes her decades-long diary but omits everything before she was thirty-four, the year of her sudden, irreversible, international fame—an appeal that she was born famous.

———

I love word games, in which words are reduced to objects, and which kill the intimacy I maintain with the same words when I'm writing.

————

There truly are two kinds of people: you and everyone else.

————

The best form isn't always the most efficient form.

————

I'm seldom bored at home, but I'm often bored while traveling. At home, where my daily routine is automatic enough that I can almost ignore it, I'm free to think about what I want.

————

It's impossible to fail if one doesn't know how the end should look. And it's impossible to succeed. But it's possible to enjoy.

———

I failed Chem 10 and gave up on becoming a physician. Then I became a chronically ill person. I know my case extremely well. I've been practicing for more than twenty years.

———

Those without taste smugly praise the thrice-belaureled. Poor taste is something else.

———

Great talents encourage great incapacities, but maintaining an inability to cook an egg or drive a car won't make you into a genius.

———

The will can achieve some things, but one must exhaust one's will in order to learn which things they are.

———

I wish someone would tell me what I should be doing instead of this, that he'd be right, and that I'd believe him.

———

Sometimes ill-informed choices have good outcomes.

———

Every success story can be told as a series of failures.

———

When a student surpasses my expectations, I feel proud and betrayed.

———

I know a woman who runs marathons she doesn't train for. Isn't that bad for your joints, or something? *You just have to be stubborn,* she says.

———

Progress takes place in the dark, when you aren't trying.

———

My long romance with efficiency has made me miserly.

———

Given a year's pay up front, I produce almost nothing. Given a month's pay, I produce what otherwise would have taken a year. Given nothing, I work when I can. Time and production must bear some relation to each other, but I couldn't say what it is.

———

There's nothing wrong with being unhappy if you don't consider unhappiness a pathology.

———

I used to have a handwriting. Now I just have a signature.

———

Achieve a goal and suffer its loss.

———

Lack of effort poorly conceals lack of ability.

———

My friend who runs marathons, throws elaborate parties, sews quilts for everyone she knows, works full-time, and has three children does all of this not in spite of her useless husband but because of him.

———

It takes time to recover from having run somewhere. But sometimes one just wants to run. Anywhere.

––––––

Someone I knew prevented me from getting a job. I fantasized about his death. Years later, he was fired publicly and shamefully. Then he was divorced. Then he developed a disabling illness. With each of his new misfortunes I'm punished further, with secret guilt, for wishing all of it on him, long ago.

––––––

After I submitted the final draft of my book about a train-track suicide, the art department produced sketches for my book cover: a needle and a long skein of red thread; a length of fluffy pinkish lace; a yellow hand mirror lying on a patch of green grass. I gave my editor a note for the designers, and the next day they delivered a perfect cover design: a photograph of the book's subject, a man sitting on a train. This was the note: *Pretend this book was written by a man.*

———

Everything has to be paid for, especially money.

———

A writer half a generation older than I am wins a huge prize and still loses his keys and his phone in the city in the rain and is taken in by an acquaintance and given supper and a bath. I was like that once, and I'm not like that anymore. I stopped showing up for that life. I miss its easy affiliation with genius.

———

Bad books sell; people have bad taste. Bad books don't sell; people prefer great books. Great books sell; after all, they are great. Great books don't sell; they are too great to be understood. Great books sell only after their authors die. We're comfortable with all of these clichés even though they can't logically coexist.

———

Think of this as a short book composed entirely of what I hoped would be a long book's quotable passages.

———

Determining when to maintain or to relinquish control is the entire job of any artist and any person. But one must learn a new type of control for every work and every relationship.

———

I notice a dangling modifier in a friend's professional bio and don't tell him. It is nothing less than sabotage.

———

Vocation and ambition are different, but ambition doesn't know the difference.

———

I was a townie and my college roommates were the daughters of famous people. Their casual confusion of social class with accomplishment, their inane preppie-Marxism, their pretense of risk by taking obscure graduate seminars, their general filth—I understood things then. Somehow I became confused in the ensuing years, and by the time I was thirty, I was living as if I were expecting an inheritance.

———

Respect the one-hit wonder not for his one hit but for all the days he must have suffered afterward, trying for another.

———

My considerate friend insists on hearing about my troubles first, and after several minutes of excavation, I'm drowning in them and can't sufficiently attend to hers. But I'm doing her a favor, letting her escape her suffering into mine.

———

Difficulty becomes familiar, at least, if no less difficult.

———

The trouble with setting goals is that you're constantly working toward what you used to want.

———

When I indulge in envy, I envy everyone who has ever achieved anything, even things I achieved fifteen years ago.

———

Worry is impatience for the next horror.

———

Once a year, the extrovert's kitchen will allow him to make an impressive five-course meal for six, but it will yield nothing when he needs to make a simple breakfast more than two days in a row.

———

When I was a pianist I had two equal and opposite fears: becoming the best and failing to become the best. Most of those who tried to be the best failed. So I tried to be the second-best, and sometimes I succeeded.

———

*I don't know myself as well as I used to,* says a middle-aged friend raising two young children. But he does know. He just isn't thinking about it as much anymore.

———

Happiness begins to deteriorate once it is named.

———

It's worth paying someone thirteen dollars to console the baby while he cries, for that's an hour I wouldn't be able to write or do anything but console the baby. But is it worth paying someone thirteen dollars while I write something that will someday be worth more than thirteen dollars if the hour I miss is the one during which the baby first smiles, first chews his hand, first laughs? Does the first time matter that much, or will the first time I see him smile be the first time that matters more than the absolute first time, for which I was not present? I'm faced at every moment with two possible lives, and I must choose one without knowing whether I want it, whether it's worth it.

———

When asked my profession, I answered *scrittore,* never *scrittrice,* and was sometimes surprised by those who didn't find it necessary to correct me.

———

Those whose every act is praised are handicapped by adoration. They grow stunted, shrivel up, lose the impulse to continue. Praise can kill.

———

The dead writer's closets held stacks of his own books and written requests for inscriptions. In the end, he couldn't even manage to sign his name.

———

Failure is good preparation for success, which comes as a pleasant surprise, but success is poor preparation for failure.

———

If I could have one wish it would be for general competence. I'd be able to drive, cook, write, and entertain with grace and ease, without having to consult an authority, apply its instruction, doubt the instruction, consult another authority, and so on. I suspect competence follows from an ability to believe oneself competent. Maybe that's what I should be wishing for instead.

———

Depression is hard to describe not just because it is complex and abstract but also because it occupies the part of us capable of describing things.

———

One woman is beautiful; the other isn't. Both are brilliant wits; one boasts a scholarly fluency. Both have earned a lot of money from their writing. Neither has children; both live alone. One of them tends toward cuteness, the other toward pedantry. I realize I don't envy them exactly; I envy a hybrid monster with some qualities of each woman but all of neither—a monster I dreamt up specifically to envy.

———

I don't envy the great writers. I envy those who believe they might be great.

———

You aren't the same person after a good night's sleep as you are after a sleepless night. But which person is you?

———

So many things I'll never try again. People my age who are still trying—I don't know where that energy comes from. Perhaps they're unhappy. Perhaps I'm happy, but I never thought happiness would feel like this.

———

Turn forty and suddenly you're too old to die tragically young, but at least you still have a chance of dying fascinatingly old.

———

Sick and tired, I try to write about being sick and tired, but my vocabulary is sparse, my associations slow and familiar. The words that come are flat of affect and connote nothing. Strapped to his chair—like me, a fall risk—the old man sits silent. His legs slap at the ground, his lifelong walking habit deeply encoded in his body. The alarm on my bed sounds if I get up, so I sit in bed and type on my keyboard, thinking nothing, my fingertips tapping out all the old familiar key sequences. The old man's body doesn't yet know any reason to stop walking, as mine doesn't yet know any reason to stop typing.

———

In sports, failure is outwardly observable, which is to say it is a sign—look, there it is, the tennis ball that bounced twice. In the rest of life, failure is mostly complex, nuanced, secret. It's a private self-judgment, a symptom you cannot observe. As with pain, I can only tell you about it.

———

Depression doesn't just steal the depressed person's capacity for joy. It throws its mantle over everything he has ever done and everything he could ever do. The depressed person dies not to save himself from the world but to save the world from himself. In this case the word *depression* makes clear sense; he is pressed down, forever.

———

There is another kind of suffering, though, a pure agony, free from thought.

———

Choose one: chronic disappointment or lowering your expectations to the point where nothing can disappoint you. But consider also that you might miss feeling disappointed.

———

I love the doctors who act unimpressed, as if everyone has to contend with this.

———

Facing death requires courage, of course, but so does facing other fears. Greater fears. I've been accused of courage for the time I've spent on intensive care units, but I was braver when I had to back a car down a steep, unlit road at night.

———

My friend's senile Catholic father blesses her: *In the name of the father, the mother, and the little boys and girls.*

———

My entire childhood was spent accompanying my parents to swap meets, yard sales, junk shops, and the dump. At a flea market I found a worn silver signet ring already engraved with my initials. Maybe someone wore it her whole life. The dealer sold it to me by weight.

———

I'd never have guessed which people I'd still know by now.

———

I fret about my lost scarf. Then I miss my flight. The scarf is no longer a problem.

———

I wouldn't argue that my life carries an intrinsic purpose other than ushering chromosomes forward in time. But absent of will, my mind derives from sensory experience emotions so powerful that they seem an almost translucent veil between me and some totalizing beauty. The northern and southern lights seem a tiny introduction to it, a reminder that it's there, behind the sky.

———

At forty, many of my college friends are either wildly successful, dead, or almost dead. That's the outcome of six thousand adolescents being told every day for four years that for them, the best and brightest, anything less than wild success is failure.

———

I heard wailing, a woman's voice. I turned to look, and as I did I heard someone standing nearby murmur that a child had gotten lost, disappeared into the enormous park. Then I saw the woman. She was running, careless of the scene she was making, carrying another child in her arms, a smaller one, too small to wander away and get lost in a park. A baby. First thought: *How terrible that she cannot kill herself.*

———

The quality that all last words share: the silence after.

———

I wish I'd known at twenty-one, when I developed a chronic illness and became suddenly alienated from my peers, that over the decades, one by one, all of them would come to join me on my island.

———

Out of the corner of my eye I glimpse a cockroach I immediately hope is a hallucination or some pathology of the eye.

———

On the page, these might look like the stones of a ruin, strewn by time and weather, but I was here.

———

I used to pursue the usual things—sex, drugs, rough neighborhoods—in order to enjoy the feeling of wasting my life, of tempting danger. Motherhood has finally satisfied that hunger. It's a self-obliteration that never stops and that no one notices.

———

For a little attention, complain a little. For a lot of attention, stop complaining.

———

Only a fire can teach you what survives a fire. No, it teaches you what can survive *that* fire.

———

Every year it feels like a greater insult when a student arrives late with no excuse. *I'm going to die so many years before you do!* I want to say, pointing to the clock.

———

When I started cracking my knuckles I was told it would produce painful arthritic swellings, but it felt so good, I kept doing it. Thirty years later, my knuckles are fine. I crack them in loving memory of the old risk.

———

I love singing in choirs, climbing out of subway tunnels onto crowded sidewalks, shedding my discreteness and disappearing into the local environment.

———

After I became a mother I became at once more and less lonely. I feel less lonely when I consider the name-

less others, the unknown billions, who have partici-
pated in this particular loneliness.

———

Not every narrative is an arc. The universe, for ex-
ample, just keeps expanding. But from the universe's
perspective, the expanding might barely have started.
Or it might be almost finished.

———

If you insist that people witness your beauty, they'll
watch it closely until it's gone.

———

I grew up amid violently white winters and green
summers and roaring autumns. Now, in a place without such seasons, I'm stuck in a waiting room with the
TV on the same channel all day, and I'm never called
in for my appointment.

———

Beside the highway are the mountains of the windward volcano, the green curtains that flutter around heaven. We see them for only a moment, so they look like stone, but the gods watch them billow in the wind.

———

What fails to kill me will kill me eventually.

———

I want to shed my fears one by one until there is nothing left of me.

———

When I lived on my own, my only experience of illness was the illness itself. It's now just as much about my son.

———

If you go to Paris, you won't find Paris; you'll find yourself in Paris. Ditto anywhere else. You might as well stay home. There, where the surrounding environment fades to neutral, you'll really find yourself, but only if you're really looking.

———

I didn't know how to knit when I joined a knitting group with a half dozen women who'd been born rich. I thought I'd learn something they all knew, but in the end I found there was nothing they all knew. There was just money.

———

There once was another Sarah Manguso. She lived in Colorado. Then she changed her name and disappeared from the Internet. I miss her.

———

The greatest commitments are to experiences with no known end points: friendship, marriage, parenthood, one's own life.

———

Once you've traveled far enough from where you began, it's impossible to reconcile the present with the past.

———

I don't miss the city. I miss the place it was in the nineties, when everyone else also was twenty-two and broke.

———

I read sad stories to inoculate myself against grief. I watch action movies to identify with the quick-witted heroes. Both the same fantasy: I'll escape the worst of it.

———

It is difficult to admit that my family is the center of my life, having spent my life insisting I didn't want children, that writing was my life's center. I just want you to join me here, in this world, where philosophically perfect, unchallenged selfhood is no longer possible.

———

Why should I leave instructions? The ashes will be my family's, not mine, the scattering their mnemonic for the idea of me.

———

Instead of pathologizing every human quirk, we should say, *By the grace of this behavior, this individual has found it possible to continue.*

———

Suddenly all eyes looked mechanical—my friend's, the waiter's, those of the other diners. Their irises had become gears. Robots surrounded me, the only living creature on Earth. I closed my own eyes for a moment and recovered, but incompletely. I can't forget how close insanity is, how easy it might be to drive off the shoulder of the road into a place where no one would ever find me.

———

Reimagine a psychiatric pathology textbook as a self-help book. *I could pull out all my hair! Maybe that would help.* When I was ten years old I pulled out all my eyelashes. It helped.

———

In a dream my friend, a real-life suicide, wants to bash my head in with a rock. I go to another room, hoping someone will notice me, but I stay silent out of loyalty or fear. They walk my friend out in chains, but I know he will return. When I wake I understand he is the specter of self-murder, chasing me.

———

I look at young people and marvel at their ignorance of what's coming, and the old people look at me.

———

Giving up hope and submitting to suffering looks the same as achieving total detachment and surpassing the Buddha but for one detail: the smile. Remember to smile.

———

After midnight in our new town, the traffic signals flash red until morning. The first time I see them I remember driving home at night when I was sixteen, the only car on the road, red lights blinking me all the way down Main Street. Windows open, no radio. The steady clicking of the lights. I hadn't remembered that in decades. That particular quiet.

———

Perfect happiness is the privilege of deciding when things end. But then you have to find a new happiness.

———

Thank you, Tanya Bezreh, Sheila Heti, Chelsea Hodson, Eli Horowitz, Miranda July, PJ Mark, Julie Orringer, James Richardson, David Shields, Zadie Smith, Marya Spence, and Lorin Stein; Ethan Nosowsky and everyone at Graywolf; and Adam and Sam, for anchoring me to the earth.

SARAH MANGUSO is the author of six previous books including *Ongoingness,* *The Guardians,* and *The Two Kinds of Decay.* Her work has been supported by a Guggenheim Fellowship and the Rome Prize.

The text of *300 Arguments* is set in Minion Pro. Book design by Ann Sudmeier. Composition by Bookmobile Design & Digital Publisher Services, Minneapolis, Minnesota. Manufactured by Friesens on acid-free, 100 percent postconsumer wastepaper.